Esther

This edition was first published in the UK in 2003 in conjunction with an advertising campaign put out by The Scottish Bible Society

SCO╫ISH
BIBLE SOCIETY
The Word for the world

7 Hampton Terrace
Edinburgh EH12 5XU
0131 337 9701

www.scottishbiblesociety.org
Cover photo Thomas Schlep
Cover design and copyright Martin Carson
This extract is from the
Holy Bible, New Living Translation,
copyright © 1996 by Tyndale Charitable Trust.
All rights reserved.
Scripture quotations are taken from the *Holy Bible*,
New Living Translation, copyright © 1996.
Used by permission of Tyndale House Publishers, Inc.,
Wheaton, Illinois 60189. All rights reserved.
New Living, and the New Living Translation logo
are registered trademarks of Tyndale House Publishers, Inc.
Arranged by Trevor Webb, Martin Casson and Chas Bayfield
Photo copyright Corbis
Design copyright Christians in Media

ISBN 0 901518 40 9

www.bookofgod.org
Website produced in association with
Lion Publishing plc
Mayfield House, 256 Banbury Road, Oxford OX2 7DH

www.lion-publishing.co.uk

The Book of God is a series of stories taken from the Bible and produced in a contemporary format for the twenty-first century. The series was the brainchild of the Scottish Bible Society and is an ideal way for people who have no formal knowledge of the Bible to dip in and sample some of the stories, poetry, wisdom, history and philosophy it contains. If you would like to own a copy of the Bible, the voucher opposite entitles you to a discount on the *Holy Bible*, New Living Translation, *The Word edition*, from the original ancient texts, a version which is designed to be easily understood by today's readers.

To see - and read – more of the stories selected by the Book of God project, visit www.bookofgod.org

Esther

Sometimes, you have to risk everything to save the ones you love, even if it means your own life.

Beautiful but vulnerable, Esther is high queen of the empire of Babylon. Orphaned as a child and taken from the family who cared for her, she was brought into the royal harem to become a sex slave for King Xerxes the Great. Despite having enormous luxury bestowed on her, Esther is homesick and lonely; an unlikely position from which to emerge as the greatest heroin of a generation.

Esther's story is one of enormous spirit and bravery; one of heroes and villains and of tragedy averted. Outwardly, she is vulnerable and weak, but through her courage and strength of will, she averts the mass genocide of her people.

Esther's story proves that it is beauty on the inside, rather than on the outside that makes the greatest difference.

The story of Esther takes place almost five hundred years before the birth of Jesus at the lowest point in Jewish history – the seventy year exile in Babylon, now part of modern day Iraq.

1

This happened in the days of King Xerxes, who reigned over 127 provinces stretching from India to Ethiopia. At that time he ruled his empire from his throne at the fortress of Susa. In the third year of his reign, he gave a banquet for all his princes and officials. He invited all the military officers of Media and Persia, as well as the noblemen and provincial officials. The celebration lasted six months - a tremendous display of the opulent wealth and glory of his empire.

When it was all over, the king gave a special banquet for all the palace servants and officials - from the greatest to the least. It lasted for seven days and was held at Susa in the courtyard of the palace garden. The courtyard was decorated with beautifully woven white and blue linen hangings, fastened by purple ribbons to silver rings embedded in marble pillars. Gold and silver couches stood on a mosaic pavement of porphyry, marble, mother-of-pearl, and other costly stones. Drinks were served in gold goblets of many designs, and there was an abundance of royal wine, just as the king had commanded. The only restriction on the drinking was that no one should be compelled to take more than he wanted. But those who wished could have as much as they pleased, for the king had instructed his staff to let everyone decide this matter for himself.

Queen Vashti gave a banquet for the women of the palace at the same time.

On the seventh day of the feast, when King Xerxes was half drunk with wine, he told Mehuman, Biztha, Harbona, Bigtha, Abagtha, Zethar, and Carcas, the seven eunuchs who attended him, to bring Queen Vashti to him with the royal crown on her head. He wanted all the men to gaze on her beauty, for she was a very beautiful woman. But when they conveyed the king's order to Queen Vashti, she refused to come. This made the king furious, and he burned with anger.

He immediately consulted with his advisers, who knew all the Persian laws and customs, for he always asked their advice. The names of these men were Carshena, Shethar, Admatha, Tarshish, Meres, Marsena, and Memucan - seven high officials of Persia and Media. They were his closest associates and held the highest positions in the empire.

"What must be done to Queen Vashti?" the king demanded. "What penalty does the law provide for a queen who refuses to obey the king's orders, properly sent through his eunuchs?" Memucan answered the king and his princes,

"Queen Vashti has wronged not only the king but also every official and citizen throughout your empire. Women everywhere will begin to despise their husbands when they learn that Queen Vashti has refused to appear before the king. Before this day is out, the wife of every one of us, your officials throughout the empire, will hear what the queen did and will start talking to their husbands the same way. There will be no end to the contempt and anger throughout your realm. So if it please the king, we suggest that you issue a written decree, a law of the Persians and Medes that cannot be revoked. It should order that Queen Vashti be forever banished from your presence and that you choose another queen more worthy than she. When this decree is published throughout your vast empire, husbands everywhere, whatever their rank, will receive proper respect from their wives!"

The king and his princes thought this made good sense, so he followed Memucan's counsel. He sent letters to all parts of the empire, to each province in its own script and language, proclaiming that every man should be the ruler of his home.

2

But after Xerxes' anger had cooled, he began thinking about Vashti and what she had done and the decree he had made. So his attendants suggested,

"Let us search the empire to find beautiful young virgins for the king. Let the king appoint agents in each province to bring these beautiful young women into the royal harem at Susa. Hegai, the eunuch in charge, will see that they are all given beauty treatments. After that, the young woman who pleases you most will be made queen instead of Vashti." This advice was very appealing to the king, so he put the plan into effect immediately.

Now at the fortress of Susa there was a certain Jew named Mordecai son of Jair. He was from the tribe of Benjamin and was a descendant of Kish and Shimei. His family had been exiled from Jerusalem to Babylon by King Nebuchadnezzar, along with King Jehoiachin of Judah and many others. This man had a beautiful and lovely young cousin, Hadassah, who was also called Esther. When her father and mother had died, Mordecai adopted her into his family and raised her as his own daughter. As a result of the king's decree, Esther, along with many other young women, was brought to the king's harem at the fortress of Susa and placed in Hegai's care. Hegai was very impressed with Esther and treated her kindly. He quickly ordered a special menu for her and provided her with beauty treatments. He also assigned her seven maids specially chosen from the king's palace, and he moved her and her maids into the best place in the harem.

Esther had not told anyone of her nationality and family background, for Mordecai had told her not to. Every day Mordecai would take a walk near the courtyard of the harem to ask about Esther and to find out what was happening to her. Before each young woman was taken to the king's bed, she was given the prescribed twelve months of beauty treatments - six months with oil of myrrh, followed by six months with special perfumes and ointments. When the time came for her to go in to the king, she was given her choice of whatever clothing or jewellery she wanted to enhance her beauty. That evening she was taken to the king's private rooms, and the next morning she was brought to the second harem, where the king's wives lived. There she would be under the care of Shaashgaz, another of the king's eunuchs. She would live there for the rest of her life, never going to the king again unless he had especially enjoyed her and requested her by name.

When it was Esther's turn to go to the king, she accepted the advice of Hegai, the eunuch in charge of the harem. She asked for nothing except what he suggested, and she was admired by everyone who saw her. When Esther was taken to King Xerxes at the royal palace in early winter of the seventh year of his reign, the king loved her more than any of the other young women. He was so delighted with her that he set the royal crown on her head and declared her queen instead of Vashti. To celebrate the occasion, he gave a banquet in Esther's honour for all his princes and servants, giving generous gifts to everyone and declaring a public festival for the provinces.

Even after all the young women had been transferred to the second harem and Mordecai had become a palace official, Esther continued to keep her nationality and family background a secret. She was still following Mordecai's orders, just as she did when she was living in his home.

One day as Mordecai was on duty at the palace, two of the king's eunuchs, Bigthana and Teresh - who were guards at the door of the king's private quarters - became angry at King Xerxes and plotted to assassinate him. But Mordecai heard about the plot and passed the information on to Queen Esther. She then told the king about it and gave Mordecai credit for the report. When an investigation was made and Mordecai's story was found to be true, the two men were hanged on a gallows. This was all duly recorded in *The Book of the History of King Xerxes' Reign.*

3

Some time later, King Xerxes promoted Haman son of Hammedatha the Agagite to prime minister, making him the most powerful official in the empire next to the king himself. All the king's officials would bow down before Haman to show him respect whenever he passed by, for so the king had commanded. But Mordecai refused to bow down or show him respect.

Then the palace officials at the king's gate asked Mordecai,

"Why are you disobeying the king's command?" They spoke to him day after day, but still he refused to comply with the order. So they spoke to Haman about this to see if he would tolerate Mordecai's conduct, since Mordecai had told them he was a Jew.

When Haman saw that Mordecai would not bow down or show him respect, he was filled with rage. So he decided it was not enough to lay hands on Mordecai alone. Since he had learned that Mordecai was a Jew, he decided to destroy all the Jews throughout the entire empire of Xerxes.

So in the month of April, during the twelfth year of King Xerxes' reign, lots were cast (the lots were called *purim*) to determine the best day and month to take action. And the day selected was March 7, nearly a year later.

Then Haman approached King Xerxes and said,

"There is a certain race of people scattered through all the provinces of your empire. Their laws are different from those of any other nation, and they refuse to obey even the laws of the king. So it is not in the king's interest to let them live. If it please Your Majesty, issue a decree that they be destroyed, and I will give 375 tons of silver to the government administrators so they can put it into the royal treasury." The king agreed, confirming his decision by removing his signet ring from his finger and giving it to

Haman son of Hammedatha the Agagite - the enemy of the Jews.

"Keep the money," the king told Haman, "but go ahead and do as you like with these people."

On April 17 Haman called in the king's secretaries and dictated letters to the princes, the governors of the respective provinces, and the local officials of each province in their own scripts and languages. These letters were signed in the name of King Xerxes, sealed with his ring, and sent by messengers into all the provinces of the empire. The letters decreed that all Jews - young and old, including women and children - must be killed, slaughtered, and annihilated on a single day. This was scheduled to happen nearly a year later on March 7. The property of the Jews would be given to those who killed them. A copy of this decree was to be issued in every province and made known to all the people, so that they would be ready to do their duty on the appointed day. At the king's command, the decree went out by the swiftest messengers, and it was proclaimed in the fortress of Susa. Then the king and Haman sat down to drink, but the city of Susa fell into confusion.

4

When Mordecai learned what had been done, he tore his clothes, put on sackcloth and ashes, and went out into the city, crying with a loud and bitter wail. He stood outside the gate of the palace, for no one was allowed to enter while wearing clothes of mourning. And as news of the king's decree reached all the provinces, there was great mourning among the Jews. They fasted, wept, and wailed, and many people lay in sackcloth and ashes.

When Queen Esther's maids and eunuchs came and told her about Mordecai, she was deeply distressed. She sent clothing to him to replace the sackcloth, but he refused it. Then Esther sent for Hathach, one of the king's eunuchs who had been appointed as her attendant. She ordered him to go to Mordecai and find out what was troubling him and why he was in mourning. So Hathach went out to Mordecai in the square in front of the palace gate.

Mordecai told him the whole story and told him how much money Haman had promised to pay into the royal treasury for the destruction of the Jews. Mordecai gave Hathach a copy of the decree issued in Susa that called for the death of all Jews, and he asked Hathach to show it to

Esther. He also asked Hathach to explain it to her and to urge her to go to the king to beg for mercy and plead for her people. So Hathach returned to Esther with Mordecai's message.

Then Esther told Hathach to go back and relay this message to Mordecai:

"The whole world knows that anyone who appears before the king in his inner court without being invited is doomed to die unless the king holds out his golden scepter. And the king has not called for me to come to him in more than a month." So Hathach gave Esther's message to Mordecai.

Mordecai sent back this reply to Esther:

"Don't think for a moment that you will escape there in the palace when all other Jews are killed. If you keep quiet at a time like this, deliverance for the Jews will arise from some other place, but you and your relatives will die. What's more, who can say but that you have been elevated to the palace for just such a time as this?" Then Esther sent this reply to Mordecai:

"Go and gather together all the Jews of Susa and fast for me. Do not eat or drink for three days, night or day. My maids and I will do the same. And then, though it is against the law, I will go in to see the king. If I must die, I am willing to die." So Mordecai went away and did as Esther told him.

5

Three days later, Esther put on her royal robes and entered the inner court of the palace, just across from the king's hall. The king was sitting on his royal throne, facing the entrance. When he saw Queen Esther standing there in the inner court, he welcomed her, holding out the golden sceptre to her. So Esther approached and touched its tip.

Then the king asked her,

"What do you want, Queen Esther? What is your request? I will give it to you, even if it is half the kingdom!" And Esther replied,

"If it please Your Majesty, let the king and Haman come today to a banquet I have prepared for the king." The king turned to his attendants and said,

"Tell Haman to come quickly to a banquet, as Esther has requested." So the king and Haman went to Esther's banquet. And while they were drinking wine, the king said to Esther, "Now tell me what you really want. What is your request? I will give it to you, even if it is half the kingdom!" Esther replied,

"This is my request and deepest wish. If Your Majesty is pleased with me and wants to grant my request, please come with Haman tomorrow to the banquet I will prepare for you. Then tomorrow I will explain what this is all about."

What a happy man Haman was as he left the banquet! But when he saw Mordecai sitting at the gate, not standing up or trembling nervously before him, he was furious. However, he restrained himself and went on home. Then he gathered together his friends and Zeresh, his wife, and boasted to them about his great wealth and his many children. He bragged about the honours the king had given him and how he had been promoted over all the other officials and leaders. Then Haman added,

"And that's not all! Queen Esther invited only me and the king himself to the banquet she prepared for us. And she has invited me to dine with her and the king again tomorrow!" Then he added, "But all this is meaningless as long as I see Mordecai the Jew just sitting there at the palace gate." So Haman's wife, Zeresh, and all his friends suggested,

"Set up a gallows that stands 23 metres tall, and in the morning ask the king to hang Mordecai on it. When this is done, you can go on your merry way to the banquet with the king." This pleased Haman immensely, and he ordered the gallows set up.

6

That night the king had trouble sleeping, so he ordered an attendant to bring the historical records of his kingdom so they could be read to him. In those records he discovered an account of how Mordecai had exposed the plot of Bigthana and Teresh, two of the eunuchs who guarded the door to the king's private quarters. They had plotted to assassinate the king.

"What reward or recognition did we ever give Mordecai for this?" the king asked. His attendants replied,

"Nothing has been done."

"Who is that in the outer court?" the king inquired. Now, as it happened, Haman had just arrived in the outer court of the palace to ask the king to hang Mordecai from the gallows he had prepared. So the attendants replied to the king,

"Haman is out there."

"Bring him in," the king ordered. So Haman came in, and the king said, "What should I do to honour a man who truly pleases me?" Haman thought to himself, "Whom would the king wish to honour more than me?" So he replied,

"If the king wishes to honour someone, he should bring out one of the king's own royal robes, as well as the king's own horse with a royal emblem on its head. Instruct one of the king's most noble princes to dress the man in the king's robe and to lead him through the city square on the king's own horse. Have the prince shout as they go, 'This is what happens to those the king wishes to honour!'"

"Excellent!" the king said to Haman. "Hurry and get the robe and my horse, and do just as you have said for Mordecai the Jew, who sits at the gate of the palace. Do not fail to carry out everything you have suggested." So Haman took the robe and put it on Mordecai, placed him on the king's own horse, and led him through the city square, shouting,

"This is what happens to those the king wishes to honour!" Afterwards Mordecai returned to the palace gate, but Haman hurried home dejected and completely humiliated. When Haman told his wife, Zeresh, and all his friends what had happened, they said,

"Since Mordecai - this man who has humiliated you - is a Jew, you will never succeed in your plans against him. It will be fatal to continue to oppose him." While they were still talking, the king's eunuchs arrived to take Haman to the banquet Esther had prepared.

7

So the king and Haman went to Queen Esther's banquet. And while they were drinking wine that day, the king again asked her, "Tell me what you want, Queen Esther. What is your request? I will give it to you, even if it is half the kingdom!" And so Queen Esther replied,

"If Your Majesty is pleased with me and wants to grant my request, my petition is that my life and the lives of my people will be spared. For my people and I have been sold to those who would kill, slaughter, and annihilate us. If we had only been sold as slaves, I could remain quiet, for that would have been a matter too trivial to warrant disturbing the king."

"Who would do such a thing?" King Xerxes demanded.

"Who would dare touch you?" Esther replied,

"This wicked Haman is our enemy." Haman grew pale with fright before the king and queen. Then the king jumped to his feet in a rage and went out into the palace garden. But Haman stayed behind to plead for his life with Queen Esther, for he knew that he was doomed. In despair he fell on the couch where Queen Esther was reclining, just as the king returned from the palace garden.

"Will he even assault the queen right here in the palace, before my very eyes?" the king roared. And as soon as the king spoke, his attendants covered Haman's face, signalling his doom. Then Harbona, one of the king's eunuchs, said,

"Haman has set up a gallows that stands 23 metres tall in his own courtyard. He intended to use it to hang Mordecai, the man who saved the king from assassination."

"Then hang Haman on it!" the king ordered. So they hanged Haman on the gallows he had set up for Mordecai, and the king's anger was pacified.

8

On that same day King Xerxes gave the estate of Haman, the enemy of the Jews, to Queen Esther. Then Mordecai was brought before the king, for Esther had told the king how they were related. The king took off his signet ring - which he had taken back from Haman - and gave it to Mordecai. And Esther appointed Mordecai to be in charge of Haman's property. Now once more Esther came before the king, falling down at his feet and begging him with tears to stop Haman's evil plot against the Jews. Again the king held out the golden sceptre to Esther. So she rose and stood before him and said,

"If Your Majesty is pleased with me and if he thinks it is right, send out a decree reversing Haman's orders to destroy the Jews throughout all the provinces of the king. For how can I endure to see my people and my family slaughtered and destroyed?"

Then King Xerxes said to Queen Esther and Mordecai the Jew,

"I have given Esther the estate of Haman, and he has been hanged on the gallows because he tried to destroy the Jews. Now go ahead and send a message to the Jews in the king's name, telling them whatever you want, and seal it with the king's signet ring. But remember that whatever is written in the king's name and sealed with his ring can never be revoked."

So on June 25 the king's secretaries were summoned. As Mordecai dictated, they wrote a decree to the Jews and to the princes, governors, and local officials of all the 127 provinces stretching from India to Ethiopia. The decree was written in the scripts and languages of all the peoples of the empire, including the Jews. Mordecai wrote in the name of King Xerxes and sealed the message with the king's signet ring. He sent the letters by swift messengers, who rode horses especially bred for the king's service.

The king's decree gave the Jews in every city authority to unite to defend their lives. They were allowed to kill, slaughter, and annihilate anyone of any nationality or province who might attack them or their children and wives, and to take the property of their enemies. The day chosen for this event throughout all the provinces of

King Xerxes was March 7 of the next year. A copy of this decree was to be recognized as law in every province and proclaimed to all the people. That way the Jews would be ready on that day to take revenge on their enemies. So urged on by the king's command, the messengers rode out swiftly on horses bred for the king's service. The same decree was also issued at the fortress of Susa.

Then Mordecai put on the royal robe of blue and white and the great crown of gold, and he wore an outer cloak of fine linen and purple. And the people of Susa celebrated the new decree. The Jews were filled with joy and gladness and were honoured everywhere. In every city and province, wherever the king's decree arrived, the Jews rejoiced and had a great celebration and declared a public festival and holiday. And many of the people of the land became Jews themselves, for they feared what the Jews might do to them.

9

So on March 7 the two decrees of the king were put into effect. On that day, the enemies of the Jews had hoped to destroy them, but quite the opposite happened.

The Jews gathered in their cities throughout all the king's provinces to defend themselves against anyone who might try to harm them. But no one could make a stand against them, for everyone was afraid of them. And all the commanders of the provinces, the princes, the governors, and the royal officials helped the Jews for fear of Mordecai. For Mordecai had been promoted in the king's palace, and his fame spread throughout all the provinces as he became more and more powerful.

But the Jews went ahead on the appointed day and struck down their enemies with the sword. They killed and annihilated their enemies and did as they pleased with those who hated them. They killed five hundred people in the fortress of Susa. They also killed Parshandatha, Dalphon, Aspatha, Poratha, Adalia, Aridatha, Parmashta, Arisai, Aridai, and Vaizatha - the ten sons of Haman son of Hammedatha, the enemy of the Jews. But they did not take any plunder.

That evening, when the king was informed of the number of people killed in the fortress of Susa, he called for Queen Esther and said,

"The Jews have killed five hundred people in the fortress of Susa alone and also Haman's ten sons. If they have done that here, what has happened in the rest of the provinces? But now, what more do you want? It will be granted to you; tell me and I will do it." And Esther said,

"If it please Your Majesty, give the Jews in Susa permission to do again tomorrow as they have done today, and have the bodies of Haman's ten sons hung from the gallows." So the king agreed, and the decree was announced in Susa. They also hung the bodies of Haman's ten sons from the gallows. Then the Jews at Susa gathered together on March 8 and killed three hundred more people, though again they took no plunder.

Meanwhile, the other Jews throughout the king's provinces had gathered together to defend their lives. They gained relief from all their enemies, killing seventy-five thousand of those who hated them. But they did not take any plunder. Throughout the provinces this was done on March 7. Then on the following day they rested, celebrating their victory with a day of feasting and gladness. But the Jews at Susa continued killing their enemies on the second day also, and then rested on the third day, making that their day of feasting and gladness. So to this day, rural Jews living in unwalled villages celebrate an annual festival and holiday in late winter, when they rejoice and send gifts to each other.

Mordecai recorded these events and sent letters to the Jews near and far, throughout all the king's provinces, encouraging them to celebrate an annual festival on these two days. He told them to celebrate these days with feasting and gladness and by giving gifts to each other and to the poor. This would commemorate a time when the Jews gained relief from their enemies, when their sorrow was turned into gladness and their mourning into joy.

So the Jews adopted Mordecai's suggestion and began this annual custom. Haman son of Hammedatha the Agagite, the enemy of the Jews, had plotted to crush and destroy them on the day and month determined by casting lots (the lots were called *purim*). But when Esther came before the king, he issued a decree causing Haman's evil plot to backfire, and Haman and his sons were hanged on the gallows. (That is why this celebration is called Purim, because it is the ancient word for casting lots.) So because of Mordecai's letter and because of what they had experienced, the Jews throughout the realm agreed to inaugurate this tradition and to pass it on to their descendants and to all who became Jews. They declared they would never fail to celebrate these two prescribed days at the appointed time each year. These days would be remembered and kept from generation to generation and celebrated by every family throughout the provinces and cities of the empire. These days would never cease to be celebrated among the Jews, nor would the memory of what happened ever die out among their descendants.

Then Queen Esther, the daughter of Abihail, along with Mordecai the Jew, wrote another letter putting the queen's full authority behind Mordecai's letter to establish the Festival of Purim. In addition, letters wishing peace and security were sent to the Jews throughout the 127 provinces of the empire of Xerxes. These letters established the Festival of Purim—an annual celebration of these days at the appointed time, decreed by both Mordecai the Jew and Queen Esther. (The people decided to observe this festival, just as they had decided for themselves and their descendants to establish the times of fasting and mourning.) So the command of Esther confirmed the practices of Purim, and it was all written down in the records.

10

King Xerxes imposed tribute throughout his empire, even to the distant coastlands. His great achievements and the full account of the greatness of Mordecai, whom the king had promoted, are recorded in *The Book of the History of the Kings of Media and Persia*. Mordecai the Jew became the prime minister, with authority next to that of King Xerxes himself. He was very great among the Jews, who held him in high esteem, because he worked for the good of his people and was a friend at the royal court for all of them.

£1.00 OFF WHEN YOU BUY
THE COMPLETE BIBLE
FROM WHICH THIS IS AN EXTRACT

To the customer: Send this voucher along with your name and address (pto) to Scottish Bible Society, Dept Ads03, 7 Hampton Terrace, Edinburgh EH12 5XU along with a cheque for £13.99.

You will be sent a copy of the full text *Holy Bible,* New Living Translation,The Word Edition, British text (This represents £1 off the retail price and postage & packing at no extra charge.)

Terms & Conditions; 1. This voucher entitles you to £1.00 off the price of the full length edition of this Bible. 2. Offer valid only through the Scottish Bible Society, subject to availability, while stocks last. 3. Voucher valid from 20 October 2003 to 17 October 2004 inclusive. 4. Cannot be exchanged for any other merchandise. 5. Only one voucher per transaction. 6. Only original, unaltered vouchers will be accepted. Cash redemption value 0.001p. Promoter: The Scottish Bible Society, 7 Hampton Terrace, Edinburgh EH12 5XU.

Name. . . . .
address. . . . .
. . . .
. . . .
Town . . . .
Post code. . . . .
Telephone . . . .
e-mail. . . . .